Filing for Bankruptcy in Iowa?

A GUIDE TO HELP YOU CHOOSE THE RIGHT CHAPTER

Shawn Smith, Esq.

ISBN: 978-1-941645-45-1

Published by:
Speakeasy Publications
73-03 Bell Blvd, #10
Oakland Gardens, NY 11364
www.SpeakeasyMarketingInc.com
(888) 225-8594

DISCLAIMER

This publication is intended to be informational only. No legal advice is being given, and no attorney-client relationship is intended to be created by reading this material. If you are facing legal issues, whether criminal or civil, seek professional legal counsel to get your questions answered.

The Smith Law Firm, PC

Ames Office
137 Lynn Avenue
Ames, IA 50014
(515) 817-1339
www.shawnsmithlaw.com

Des Moines Office
699 Walnut Street
Suite 400, 4th Floor
Des Moines, Iowa 50309
Toll Free: (855) 451-1260

Testimonials

"I had a fantastic experience with Shawn and the staff at the Smith Law Firm. Anna was always very friendly and helpful when I called and Shawn was extremely patient and non-judgmental in explaining everything to me and answering any of my additional questions. I would highly recommend The Smith Law Firm to anyone in search of legal counsel." **- Tara F.**

"Shawn is very professional. I was very pleased to work with him." **- Patty D.**

Table Of Contents

AUTHOR INTRODUCTION

Attorney Shawn Smith represents clients in the Iowa District and Appellate Courts, Iowa Northern and Southern District Federal Courts, and the Northern and Southern District Bankruptcy Courts for the State of Iowa. Additionally, he takes pride in taking on a number of Pro Bono Publico cases each year.

He looks forward to working personally with each client to fully understand and appreciate their situation, lay out the right legal strategy, and obtain the most desirable outcome.

In addition to bankruptcy/consumer law, the Smith Law Firm handles litigation and estate planning services. For other legal issues, The Smith Law Firm will gladly provide an appropriate referral for you.

Attorney Shawn Smith is committed to his client's individual legal needs. He promises to work hard to get the results that they deserve.

MEMBERSHIPS

- American Bar Association
- National Association of Criminal Defense Lawyers
- American Association of Justice
- Iowa State Bar Association
- Iowa Legal Aid Advisory Council
- Story County Bar Association
- National Institute of Certified Estate Planners

BAR ADMISSIONS

- State of Iowa
- State of Minnesota (inactive)
- U.S. District Courts, Northern and Southern District of Iowa
- U.S. Bankruptcy Courts, Northern and Southern District of Iowa
- U.S. Court of Appeals – 8th Circuit

BANKRUPTCY

There are two types of consumer bankruptcy: Chapter 7 and Chapter 13. Each is intended to help consumers in financial stress, but the solutions offered are very different.

All bankruptcy filings involve a complicated set of rules and requirements that must be followed to the letter to ensure that debtors emerge with the fresh financial start they need. Prior to submitting forms to the court, prospective bankruptcy filers must complete an accredited debt counseling program designed to help them better understand debt, and avoid the practices that caused their initial financial difficulties.

Our bankruptcy attorney works closely with you to make sure you meet all of the requirements under bankruptcy law. We make sure your filing completely addresses all outstanding debt, and provide advice that addresses any debt that cannot be wiped clean through bankruptcy.

What Is A Chapter 7 Bankruptcy?

Chapter 7 bankruptcy is often misunderstood. As a result there are a lot of myths about what a Chapter 7 is, and about what happens in a Chapter 7 bankruptcy proceeding.

Some of the common myths out there about bankruptcy are you cannot keep your home or your car, stop foreclosure, or get relief from medical debts. Again, these are all MYTHS that are NOT true.

Bankruptcy is a legal proceeding that takes place outside of a traditional court room. Essentially, it's a process where debtor asks the trustee and the bankruptcy court for total relief by liquidating and discharging most, if not all, debt. In Chapter 7, the Bankruptcy Court discharges all types of unsecured debt provided you meet the qualifications.

Qualification For A Chapter 7 Bankruptcy

Often times, there are some misunderstandings about what is required to file for a Chapter 7 bankruptcy protection. There are two basic requirements. First, any person who wishes to file for Chapter 7 must reside, own any type of property, or have some type of business in the United States. Second, a person must complete a credit counseling course from an approved agency within six months of filing for Chapter 7 bankruptcy protection.

Many credit counseling courses are available online, are easily accessible, and relatively inexpensive.

Another big misconception is that you have to be completely broke to file for Chapter 7.

This is another myth that is not true. You do not have to be insolvent to file for Chapter 7 bankruptcy protection but there are some income qualifications. There is the means test which is a provision in the bankruptcy code that is used to determine whether a presumption of abuse exists. This is based on the debtor's ability to repay the creditors and applies to those debtors whose current monthly income is above the state median income for their state. The means test focuses on the current monthly income defined as the debtor's average monthly income for the six months prior to filing for the bankruptcy. If their monthly income exceeds their state monthly income for the number of people in their household then they are subject to the test. There are some exceptions however.

Chapter 7 Bankruptcy Exemption Rules For The State Of Iowa

For some people, the exemption rules are the Holy Grail of Bankruptcy and are the key underlying factors that help people make the decision whether or not to file bankruptcy.

There are two types of exemption provisions, one under the standard bankruptcy code and the other under state law exemptions that relate to execution and garnishment. Both give a debtor tremendous rights in relation to their assets and property. These are different types of exemptions. Often, the provisions in the bankruptcy code are more extensive, enabling filers to keep much more of their assets than would be permitted under the state law exemptions.

Also, the availability of exemptions is usually key to whether to file a bankruptcy in the first place, as well as the decision which type of bankruptcy case to file. For example, if a debtor has a lot of property that is not exempt under the bankruptcy code or state law, then a Chapter 7 filing may not be the best option because they may be forced to convert the non-exempt property to cash and use to pay off creditors. A Chapter 13 filing may be the preferable course of action under those circumstances. In many states, a debtor may choose from two sets of exemptions. A debtor in any state may utilize the exemptions provided by state law, as enhanced by the bankruptcy code and the exemptions provided by other federal laws outside of the

bankruptcy code. Whether to avail one of the state exemptions or the exemptions within the bankruptcy code should be closely scrutinized and one should consult a competent professional regarding this decision. Under Iowa law the specific property exemptions are listed in Iowa Code section 627.6.

If you own multiple properties or have several assets that are not exempt under the bankruptcy code exemption or state law provisions, then Chapter 7 may not be the best option for you because those nonexempt assets will probably need to be sold and used to pay some of your creditors. In that case, a Chapter 13 may be the better course of action to take because you will enter into a payment plan with reduced payments that will allow you to retain all of your property and assets.

Before you decide whether to file Chapter 7 or 13, it is important to review and compare the types and availability of exemptions under state law and the bankruptcy code with a local bankruptcy attorney.

Bankruptcy Laws That Protect You

If you are seeking relief from excessive debt and creditors' collection actions, here are some answers to common questions about Chapter 7 bankruptcy, and how they protect you during and after the bankruptcy process.

What Is The Bankruptcy Court's Control Over Your Financial Affairs In A Chapter 7?

When you file Chapter 7 bankruptcy, you are requesting relief from debt repayment. During bankruptcy, activities related to those debts essentially stop. That means that you should not:

- Obtain new debt
- Pay off existing debt
- Buy, sell, or give property away

Most of your debts will be discharged and some of your assets will be liquidated, so the bankruptcy court must have access to all assets and be able to account for your debts. The way they do that is by creating a bankruptcy estate which owns and can sell assets, and pay or manage debts on your behalf. This ensures that any secured creditors are paid and that unsecured debts are properly discharged.

What Is An Automatic Stay Related To Bankruptcy?

Not only does the bankruptcy court exercise control over your affairs, but they also have control over what actions creditors can take against you. Once your Chapter 7 is filed, the bankruptcy court issues an automatic stay which stops many collection activities including lawsuits, liens, foreclosures, and evictions. There are some exceptions, and creditors can apply to the court for relief from the automatic stay. This gives the court time to review your assets and debts. The automatic stay gives you relief from collection actions, and legal or financial penalties while waiting for your discharge.

What Happens If A Person Files For Bankruptcy, And They Had A Co-Signor On Their Loan? How Does It Impact The Co-Signor?

If you file bankruptcy individually, only your debts will be discharged. In the case of a married couple, they can file a joint bankruptcy petition to have joint accounts discharged. When the co-signor is not filing bankruptcy, your creditors may continue collection activities against the co-signor, even after you have been discharged and are no longer personally obligated to repay the debt.

There are options you have to protect your co-signor, and your relationship with them. You can reaffirm the joint account. When you reaffirm a debt you will:

- Sign a new agreement with the lender and co-signor
- Continue to make payments during the bankruptcy process
- Waive your right to have your portion of the debt discharged

Remember that when you reaffirm a debt, the lender will be able to resume collection activity against you after the bankruptcy has been discharged.

How Much Influence Does The Cause Of A Person's Financial Situation Factor Into The Outcome Of Their Chapter 7 Bankruptcy Case?

It depends. Not all types of debts can be discharged in a Chapter 7 bankruptcy case. Here is a list of debts that generally cannot be discharged:

- Any debts not listed on the filing forms
- Alimony
- Child support
- Taxes
- Student loans
- Court-ordered restitution
- Debts arising from intentional injury to another person or destruction of property
- Debts arising from death or injury caused by DUI or DWI
- Debts obtained through fraud

Additionally, secured debt such as mortgage and auto loans will not be eligible for discharge. If your situation has been caused by these types of debts, Chapter 7 may not provide relief from debt. Therefore, you should consult with a bankruptcy attorney before filing a petition.

What Happens At The Very End Of A Bankruptcy? How Do You Know When Everything Is Finished?

From filing to discharge, the Chapter 7 bankruptcy process can last anywhere from 3 to 6 months. Both you and your creditors will receive official notification from the bankruptcy court of all discharged debts. Consider the process finished when you receive your discharge letter. At that point, your financial affairs are no longer within the control of the bankruptcy court. If you have reaffirmed debt to keep your property, you will continue to make your mortgage and car payments. For debts that have been discharged, you will not need to communicate with the creditors.

The end of the Chapter 7 bankruptcy process marks a new beginning for you. You can start the process of recovering financially and rebuilding your credit.

WHAT TYPES OF DEBT ARE DISCHARGED UNDER A CHAPTER 7 BANKRUPTCY?

The final step in a Chapter 7 bankruptcy is usually granting the debtor's discharge. To become eligible to receive a Chapter 7 discharge and relinquishment of debt, a bankruptcy filer must, with very limited exceptions, complete a personal financial management course through an approved provider. This instructional course can be taken in person, by telephone, or online. You must complete the course within sixty days after the first date set for the meeting of creditors. A Chapter 7 discharge can eliminate the legal obligation to pay most or all of your debts. The bankruptcy filing and discharge can prevent repossession of your car or other property. In some cases, your property can be returned to you if it was already repossessed. It can stop wage garnishments, and other types of levies on accounts. Also, it can stop harassment from creditors attempting to collect debts. Granting a discharge in a Chapter 7 bankruptcy can offer enormous benefits to a debtor drowning in debt and truly give one the relief they need by providing them with a fresh start.

Most unsecured debts will be discharged however; there are some things that a Chapter 7 will not discharge. Typically what a Chapter 7 cannot discharge are debts like child support, alimony or any type of criminal restitution orders or fines. Most taxes and any debts owed to any creditor that is not listed on a bankruptcy schedule will not be discharged. Debt incurred through false pretenses or fraud is not eligible for discharge. Marital property settlements or any other settlement debts pursuant to a divorce may not be able to be discharged. Additionally, student loans generally are not dischargeable in a Chapter 7 proceeding, although there are some exceptions to that rule.

Can Taxes Ever Be Discharged Under A Chapter 7 Bankruptcy?

In general, taxes are not dischargeable in bankruptcy proceedings but there are some exceptions. Here is a list of tax debts that are not dischargeable in a Chapter 7 proceeding.

- Taxes due on returns that were filed within 2 years of your bankruptcy filing date
- Taxes due on income earned from regular employment or gross receipts from your business
- Property taxes that came due just prior to your filing date
- Most types of excise taxes

What Assets Am I Able To Retain After Chapter 7 Bankruptcy?

A debtor will be able to keep all exempt, non-encumbered property assets. Non-encumbered property is basically property that does not have a security interest attached to it, such as mortgage or car loan. Although the bankruptcy code does not specifically define exempt property, the property the person or debtor is able to keep often depends on one's choice of using the set of exemptions under the bankruptcy code or exemptions under state law. The property that can be claimed as exempt, is listed specifically in the bankruptcy code based on Section 522(d). These items include your home and car, furniture and appliances, clothing and jewelry, life and health insurance benefits, and disability and retirement income benefits. This list is not exhaustive and one must remember there may be value qualifications for these exemptions. For a more detailed analysis and information regarding the types and amounts of property one may keep one should consult with an Iowa bankruptcy attorney.

Is Filing For Bankruptcy Detrimental To My Financial Future?

In most cases, the answer is no, filing bankruptcy is not detrimental. Rather it helps you to plan for a more successful financial future. Typically within twelve months after filing, credit scores start to improve because bankruptcy provides a fresh start. Remember, bankruptcy discharge relieves you of the financial burden you were in, allows you to start over, and helps you rebuild a better credit profile. I have seen situations where, after about two years, a person's credit score improved by such a considerable amount that they actually had established good credit.

How Does The Bankruptcy Court Deal With My Assets?

When you file a Chapter 7, you are eligible to have most of your unsecured debts discharged. But if you have secured debts, own a home, or a vehicle then there are some important items you need to know about how the court handles your assets in Chapter 7 bankruptcy.

I've Heard It's Harder To Qualify For Chapter 7 Bankruptcy Nowadays? Is This True?

Not necessarily. Any person who lives, owns property, or operates a business in the United States is eligible to file for Chapter 7 bankruptcy protection. But some changes have occurred that you need to be aware of.

First, in 2005 the "means test" was established under the U.S. bankruptcy code to prevent higher income persons from abusing bankruptcy laws. If your income exceeds your state's median income level, the bankruptcy means test may apply. However, if your income is below your state's median, the means test is not applicable. Additionally, there are safe harbor provisions in place that exempt most people from the means test.

Second, even without the means test, the bankruptcy judge can dismiss your case if he or she determines that the filing is an abuse of the Chapter 7 bankruptcy provisions. So, while it is not harder to qualify for bankruptcy, it is important to understand the provisions and consult an attorney to decide if Chapter 7 or another bankruptcy type is right for you.

Will All Of My Unsecured Debts Be Wiped Out In Chapter 7 Bankruptcy?

Here are some of the most common types of unsecured debts that can be discharged in a Chapter 7 bankruptcy:

- Medical bills
- Past due rent (including late fees and other monies owed under lease agreements)
- Utility bills (past due amounts only)
- Collection agency accounts
- Personal loans from friends, family, and employers
- Dishonored NSF checks (unless based on fraud)
- Auto repossession deficiency balances
- Credit card charges (including overdue and late fees)
- Revolving charge accounts (except extended payment charges)

- Business-related debts

In some cases, these unsecured debts can also be discharged:

- Student loans (only in a few rare circumstances)
- Auto accident claims (except those involving DUI or DWI)
- Civil court judgments (unless based on fraud)
- Tax penalties and unpaid taxes past a certain number of years
- Attorney fees (except child support and alimony awards)
- Social security overpayments
- Veteran's assistance loans and overpayments.

It is important to note that only those debts incurred before your bankruptcy filing are dischargeable. Any new debt you incur after the bankruptcy process begins will likely not be discharged. Make sure that you list all debts from all sources. For example, if a creditor charged off and placed your account in collections, you must list both the original creditor and the collection agency in your schedule of debts.

Does A Person Have Any Options Regarding The Liquidation Of Secured Debt In A Chapter 7 Bankruptcy?

Secured debt includes such things as auto loans and real estate mortgages. Chapter 7 bankruptcy gives you options depending on whether you want to keep your home and car, or if you want your debt discharged. To keep your property, you must sign a reaffirmation agreement with the original lender and the court. This means you will continue to make payments and the lender retains all collection, repossession, and foreclosure rights if you default on your loan. If you want relief from the debt, the bankruptcy court will sell your assets to pay off the secured creditors, and often any deficiency balances can be discharged.

If I'm Current On My Mortgage, Can I Keep My Home In A Chapter 7 Bankruptcy?

Usually you can keep your home when you file Chapter 7, especially if you have no equity and are current on your mortgage payments. When the mortgage balance and other liens against your home exceed the property value, the bankruptcy court may abandon and not sell it. If there is not enough equity to pay all lienholders, the court will let you keep your home. However, the mortgage lender will retain all collection and foreclosure rights. If you are current on your mortgage payments, it is important to remain current during and after the bankruptcy process because the lender always has the right to take back the property, in foreclosure, if you default on the mortgage payment.

Keep in mind that the bankruptcy court allows you to keep your primary residence. If you also own rental property, you may not be able to keep those properties if you choose a Chapter 7 bankruptcy.

What Is The Usual Process, A Chapter 7 Trustee Will Follow, To Sell A Debtor's Home If There Is Significant Non-Exempt Equity?

If your home does have enough equity to pay off the mortgage and secured liens, the bankruptcy trustee can sell the property. With a few exceptions, the trustee uses the same method to sell the property as you would. Usually, the trustee will list the property through a real estate broker or agent, or sometimes can sell the property through an auction. They may choose an auction to sell vacant land, abandoned properties, or other real estate that may not have enough value to fully pay off lienholders. In this case, a buyer will accept the property with some liens attached. The trustee must get the court's approval to list the property and will need a court order to authorize the sale. All lienholders will be notified of the court's intention to sell the property. The mortgage company and lienholders may file an objection to the sale of the property. If the court allows the sale, all lienholders will be paid, and you must arrange to move out of your home.

Will The Debtor Ever Receive Proceeds From The Sale Of Their Home?

Sometimes you can petition the bankruptcy court to sell the property yourself. But you will need court approval and you must provide the court with a plan to administer the proceeds from the sale. You cannot keep any funds from the sale of your property because the bankruptcy court will require that the sale proceeds pay off secured lienholders first, and then to pay off other debts.

Before you file for bankruptcy, decide if you want to keep your home and car. If you own other types of property, consult with a bankruptcy attorney to make sure that Chapter 7 provides the best options for you.

The bankruptcy hearing is the most important phase of the Chapter 7 bankruptcy process. What happens during and after the hearing will depend on the types of debt you owe, if you own any property, and whether or not your creditors have any secured claims against your assets.

What Is The Purpose Of The Hearing Before The Chapter 7 Bankruptcy Trustee?

The purpose of the 341 hearing, or the meeting of creditors, is to give the bankruptcy trustee the opportunity to question you, under oath, about your financial situation and the reason for filing bankruptcy. This meeting gives you the opportunity to provide documentation of your assets and debts and to confirm the accuracy of the financial information you provided in your original Chapter 7 bankruptcy filing. You will need to bring a copy of your bankruptcy filing paperwork, a valid ID, tax returns, social security documentation, bank statements, and any information regarding the property you own like vehicle titles and real estate deeds.

When And Where Does The Hearing Before The Chapter 7 Bankruptcy Trustee Take Place?

The hearing will happen anywhere from 21 to 40 days after you file your bankruptcy petition. You will receive written notice of the time and location of the hearing, which usually takes place in the federal building where the bankruptcy court is located. Most likely, you will meet in a conference room instead of a courtroom. The bankruptcy trustee, you, your attorney, your creditors, and their attorneys can all attend the meeting of creditors.

What Actually Happens At The Meeting Of Creditors?

The bankruptcy trustee and the creditors can question you during the meeting. Be prepared to answer questions from the trustee such as:

- Why are you filing bankruptcy?
- Have you paid off any creditors within 3 months of filing for bankruptcy?
- Do you own a home, car, or business?
- What is your marital status, and do you owe any alimony or child support?
- What are your monthly income and living expenses?

Once you present all of your financial information and answer the bankruptcy trustees and creditors' questions, the trustee will determine if you have non-exempt property that can be sold to pay off debts, which debts are priority liens, and which ones are unsecured.

Do Creditors Actually Show Up?

Secured creditors or their attorneys often attend the meeting of creditors. Some unsecured creditors may also choose to attend, but typically do not. Your creditors can question you only about your accounts with them. A car lender or mortgage company can ask if you intend to keep your property and if you plan

to continue making timely payments. They may also have you sign a reaffirmation agreement so you can keep your property. Unsecured creditors may attend the meeting to ask you about accounts you opened or charges you made just prior to filing bankruptcy.

What Generally Happens After The Meeting?

After the meeting of creditors, the bankruptcy trustee will decide if you need to provide additional documentation or information to the bankruptcy court, if you have significant assets, and if you have non-exempt assets that can be sold. If the trustee needs no further information and you have no significant assets, the meeting will be concluded and you can wait to receive your discharge from the bankruptcy court. If you have significant assets the trustee will begin the liquidation process, sell your assets, and pay off your creditors. After all secured creditors are paid, the trustee will then forward your case to the bankruptcy court for discharge of the remaining unsecured debts.

UNDERSTANDING THE ROLE OF THE BANKRUPTCY TRUSTEE

The bankruptcy trustee has a 3-fold role. First, the trustee will make sure that you comply with all bankruptcy laws and codes. Second, he or she will ensure that only valid creditor claims are submitted. Third, the trustee will ensure that assets are liquidated and priority claims are paid.

What Are The Duties Of A Trustee In A Chapter 7 Bankruptcy Case?

When you file a Chapter 7, the bankruptcy court creates an estate. This is where any property you own is placed temporarily while the court determines how to liquidate non-exempt assets and pay off secured creditors and priority lienholders. The trustee's job is to sell your assets and pay your creditors. To do this, the bankruptcy trustee performs these primary duties:

- Review the bankruptcy filing paperwork and documentation
- Have a hearing to examine and question the person or persons filing for bankruptcy protection, under oath

- Avoid preferential transfers of property and security interests
- Liquidate or sell non-exempt property and assets

What Is The Trustee Looking For In The Debtor's Petition And Schedules?

The bankruptcy trustee will review your petition and verify the financial information and disclosures you provide to the court. It's the trustee's duty to verify the accuracy of your information and to make sure there is no fraud or intent to abuse the protections provided under U.S. bankruptcy law. The trustee will determine if you owe back child support. If so, they will notify the appropriate child support enforcement agency of your status throughout the bankruptcy process and at discharge. The bankruptcy trustee will also determine if your assets are exempt or non-exempt, and if your debts are secured or unsecured. The trustee will either file a no-asset report with the bankruptcy court or will notify creditors with valid liens of their right to file claims with the bankruptcy court.

What Authority/Power Does A Trustee Have In A Chapter 7 Bankruptcy Case?

The most important duties and authority of the bankruptcy trustee are dealing with security interests and liquidating assets. The trustee can do 3 things in relation to security interests. If you transferred property to, or paid off, certain individuals or creditors before filing bankruptcy, the bankruptcy trustee may be able to recover that property through the bankruptcy estate for proper distribution to priority lienholders. Alternatively, if a creditor fails to file the correct liens and timely claims, the bankruptcy trustee can sell an asset free and clear of the original lien. Where there are non-exempt assets, the bankruptcy trustee will liquidate or sell them and pay off as many creditors as possible. Once all secured claims are handled, the trustee will use any additional monies to offset the claims of unsecured creditors. In other words, the bankruptcy trustee has the authority to determine which creditors get paid and how much each one will receive.

What Would Lead A Bankruptcy Trustee To Object To A Proof Of Claim Filed By A Creditor?

Unsecured creditors can file a proof of claim if they wish to be paid from the sale of your assets. You, the bankruptcy trustee, or any interested party can file an objection to a proof of claim by a creditor. The trustee may object to a proof of claim if the lender:

- Fails to provide adequate proof of security interest such as providing copies of title, deed, liens, or UCC-1 statements.
- Files inaccurate or false priority claims.
- Files claims late.
- Fails to properly amend a claim.

If a creditor opposes the objection to their proof of claim, the bankruptcy trustee will hold a hearing. Otherwise, if the creditor's proof of claim is disallowed, they will not receive priority status when assets are sold.

Under What Circumstances, Can A Trustee Object To A Discharge?

Under normal circumstances, when there are no assets, your bankruptcy will be immediately discharged. If there are assets involved, you will receive your discharge after all assets are sold and priority lienholders are paid. The bankruptcy trustee or a creditor can object to the discharge. However, a creditor can only object to the discharge of their debt.

The trustee can object to the discharge of a single item or to all debt in a Chapter 7 bankruptcy case. The most common reason the bankruptcy trustee might object to a discharge is on the basis of fraud. Bankruptcy fraud most commonly involves hiding assets by transferring ownership prior to filing bankruptcy. Other forms of fraud include providing false information, filing multiple bankruptcy petitions in different jurisdictions, and attempting to bribe bankruptcy court officials, although this is less common. If the trustee files an objection to a discharge, you will have a hearing or trial where the trustee must provide proof of fraud and give the bankruptcy court valid reasons for the objection. If the bankruptcy judge agrees, your discharge will be denied.

How Is A Bankruptcy Trustee Compensated In A Chapter 7 Case?

The bankruptcy trustee will be paid an administrative fee and possibly receive commissions based on disbursements to creditors. The trustee will receive an administrative fee from the bankruptcy court filing fee you paid. The trustee can also receive commissions based on the amounts paid to creditors after the sale of your non-exempt assets. Based on a sliding commission scale, the trustee may receive:

- 25% of the initial $5,000 paid to creditors
- 10% from $5,001 up to $50,000
- 5% from $50,001 up to $1,000,000
- 3% over $1,000,000

If you have a no asset bankruptcy case, no commissions can be paid. Additionally, if you were granted a waiver of bankruptcy filing fees then no administrative fees will be paid either.

What Is A Chapter 13 Bankruptcy?

Chapter 13 bankruptcy is similar to a debt repayment plan. However, unlike most repayment plans, a Chapter 13 payment plan may not require you to pay off all your debt. If you file for a Chapter 13 payment plan, you will pay off some of your-past due and current debt over a period of 36 to 60 months. The remaining debts will be discharged like a Chapter 7.

Where Chapter 13 differs is in dealing with nonexempt property. Since you are in a repayment plan, you will not need to turn over your property to be sold by the bankruptcy court. Even though you are making partial or reduced payments under Chapter 13, you are still making the agreed upon payment to the creditors toward your property or other assets. One of the most important benefits of Chapter 13 is that you will be able to keep your most vital assets, your home and your car. The payment plan allows you to cure any default balances or deficiency amounts that may have accumulated.

Qualifying For Chapter 13 Bankruptcy

Similar to Chapter 7 bankruptcy, the debtor must take a credit counseling course from an approved provider within 180 days or 6 months of filing. An individual debtor must have a stable income that is adequate

enough to allow for regular payments toward the Chapter 13 repayment plan. However unlike a Chapter 7, to be eligible to file Chapter 13, an individual must not have debt in excess of, $394,725. This figure is current as of the time of publication and is subject to change. Consult a bankruptcy attorney for the most current guidelines. This also includes non-contingent liquidated unsecured debts, or over $1.1 million of non-contingent liquidated secured debts. Also an individual may not file for Chapter 13 protection if they have had a bankruptcy case that was dismissed within the previous six months.

What Types Of Debt Can Be Discharged Under A Chapter 13 Bankruptcy?

Upon completion of all payments under the Chapter 13 plan, you will be entitled to a discharge. It relieves you of any further obligation on all debts provided for in the plan, with the exception of those items specifically disallowed by the bankruptcy code. Like a Chapter 7 discharge, alimony or child support, certain taxes, and secured debts are not dischargeable. Also, it is important to note that you must certify that any domestic support obligations are current or paid in full before a discharge is allowed. Although the discharge in a Chapter 13 case is many times broader than a Chapter 7 case, there are still several types of debts that are not dischargeable such as:

- Long-term debts with final payments due after completing the plan cured in the plan such as a mortgage;
- Debts incurred through false pretenses or fraud;
- Certain tax debts;
- Debts not listed in the bankruptcy;
- Debts for fraud as a fiduciary;
- Domestic support obligations;
- Most student loan debts;
- Certain drunk driving debts;
- Certain criminal fines and restitution orders;
- Debts for damages awarded in a civil action because of willful or malicious conduct by the debtor that caused personal injury or death.

What Assets Can Be Retained In A Chapter 13 Bankruptcy?

If you choose a Chapter 13 repayment plan, you will be able to keep your property including your home, your car, and any other assets used as collateral for secured debt. When you have nonexempt assets, you may be required to pay more toward the unsecured portion of debt during your repayment period.

What Is The Major Difference Between Chapter 7 And Chapter 13 Bankruptcy?

The major difference between Chapter 7 and 13 is how your assets are handled.

In Chapter 7, you are asking the bankruptcy court to discharge all unsecured debts and provide you relief from any further repayment. With the exception of nonexempt assets and debts that are reaffirmed, certain property and assets must be sold and secured creditors paid in order to qualify for total debt relief. Chapter 7 is a faster and easier option for those who do not own any property.

Compare that to Chapter 13, where you enter into a partial debt repayment plan agreed upon by you, the creditors, and the court. Since you continue to make payments, you do not have to worry about any of your assets being sold to pay priority creditor claims. Chapter 13 allows you to retain all of your assets while making reduced payments.

How Do You Determine Which Bankruptcy Chapter Is Suitable For A Client?

When I consult with clients, I find out where they are in the debt cycle. Are they severely delinquent and on the verge of default? Or, are they already in default on multiple debts and on the verge of foreclosure and repossession?

I advise clients that Chapter 7 is the better, and more commonly used, option for someone who has little or no property beyond the basic necessities like clothing, furniture and household appliances. Chapter 7 is also the better option if you have little to no money left over after paying your expenses each month.

On the other hand, if you have quite a bit of secured debt, I advise clients to look into Chapter 13. You may have significant equity in your primary residence and want to continue living your home because it is a great family neighborhood and you want to keep your children in a good school system. Or, if you own rental properties or

other types of real estate, you can ensure that you can keep all your property by filing Chapter 13. If you have regular income and can pay your living expenses with ease, but it is a stretch to try to keep up with your scheduled debt payments, Chapter 13 gives you the option to cure any existing default and keep from falling any further into default.

So, it just depends on the particular situation of each individual. The decision to file for bankruptcy is not an easy one to make without solid information and careful guidance. At the Smith Law Firm, we always seek the best possible short and long term outcome for each and every person we meet with.

Is Filing For A Chapter 7 Better In Terms Of Credit Score Than A Chapter 13?

Chapter 13 and Chapter 7 will stay on your credit report for the same amount of time and that is about ten years. They both have typically the same effect on your credit score. However, where they diverge is, if you are applying for credit and a particular creditor is reviewing your credit report trying to decide whether to lend you money to purchase a car or a home, or approve a credit card application, they may look at a

Chapter 13 more or less favorably than the other. For example, a creditor may be more willing to lend you money or approve a loan for you if you filed for Chapter 13, which is the payment plan that shows that you are willing and able to make timely payments, and have done so consistently over three years or up to five years you have been in the Chapter 13 payment plan.

Can You Discuss The Stigma Attached With Filing For Bankruptcy?

Although bankruptcy is a legal proceeding, it is also a very emotional time as well. But, a bankruptcy discharge does provide a way to make some major life improvement after you file. Think about it in terms of value. First, consider the amount of stress you can get rid of when you don't have to deal with creditor harassment and questionable collection agency tactics.

Second, there have been a lot of divorces because of finances. Sometimes when the financial situation improves, many of the other marital problems automatically work themselves out. So, bankruptcy discharge can help you restore harmony in your family and relationships. Since bankruptcy can help you save your home from foreclosure, you and your family can feel more secure knowing that they don't have to lose their home.

Third, bankruptcy can often be a motivator or at least help you set some achievable financial goals. Your credit score can improve within twelve months of your discharge date. Completing the credit course and starting with a clean slate is not only motivating but empowering for people who are really trying and improve their financial management skills and approach credit with a fresh start.

General Human Reaction To Filing For Bankruptcy

The reaction is two-fold. Filing a bankruptcy does offer peace of mind to people with a lot of debt. However, the decision to file bankruptcy also creates a moral dilemma for many people. Some people feel like they are drowning in debt, and that is emotionally overwhelming. Being empowered with the ability to stop a creditor's relentless collection efforts can bring psychological relief to many as soon as they file for bankruptcy.

But I also know that many people harbor a lot of personal and emotional guilt about their financial situations. Historically speaking there has been a lot of shame and stigma associated with filing for bankruptcy. Fortunately, there has been a more recent move away from looking at a bankruptcy in negative light. Society no longer treats those who file bankruptcy as failures. More and more we have learned to place more value on the fresh start that bankruptcy gives to people in financial distress, often through no fault of their own. And most important: people, companies, and organizations want to help provide opportunities for people who have had to file bankruptcy to get back on track.

Have You Seen Any Success Stories In Regard To Filing For Bankruptcy?

Here is my idea of success after bankruptcy:

- not having a financial burden, stress, or constant worry;
- not having the collectors constantly calling your home phone, your work phone;
- not worrying about having your wages garnished or being sued in small claims in court;
- not worrying about whether you can qualify for a home mortgage or a car loan.

How Does Bankruptcy Affect My Credit Score?

Filing bankruptcy will most definitely have an effect on your credit score. A Chapter 7 bankruptcy will typically stay on a person's credit record for 10 years. With each passing year the effect that any item included in the bankruptcy will have on an overall credit score will decrease.

How Long Will Bankruptcy Stay On My Credit Report?

In a Chapter 7 bankruptcy recognition of the bankruptcy will stay on a person's credit report for 10 years.

How Soon Will I Be Able To Get Loan Or Credit After I File For Bankruptcy?

There are no set rules in relation to how long it takes to rebuild a person's credit score after a Chapter 7 bankruptcy is filed. If the person is able to keep their home through the bankruptcy then it would help to maintain all mortgage payments on time, that way there is something to show for creditworthiness after the bankruptcy is over. You may want to have a savings account and have a credit balance in that account as well as pay bills on time. If you have a credit card it is recommended to either not use it at all or pay any purchases off immediately. If you do not have a credit card at all, you may want to apply for a secured card shortly after the bankruptcy ends and make sure to keep up all the payments.

When Will I Be Able To Rent An Apartment Or Buy A Home Or Car?

Renting a home is possible after a bankruptcy ends although it may be the case that you will have to take a rental that is not your optimal choice. That is not always the case of course, and you should deal head on with this problem by speaking to the rental management company and explaining the terms of your bankruptcy and your ability to pay for rental payments ongoing. You may need to show that you are past the credit crunch by taking an alternative accommodation and continuing to pay rent payments on time for a period of 6 to 12 months. In order to buy a home or a car it will be necessary to build up savings while making regular payments to show that you have the ability to make ongoing payments on time again and that you have some cash to secure the loan with.

Will A Bankruptcy Affect My Eligibility For Receiving Student Loans?

Since there are different types of student loans the requirements for each type are not the same. It is possible to take federal student loans out after a bankruptcy as the ability to borrow federally backed loans should not have been affected unless there was a delinquency on a prior federal student loan. School loan programs and private loans for education will be affected by a bankruptcy the same as any other type of loan.

How Soon After A Bankruptcy Should I Start Trying To Rebuild My Credit?

You should start trying to rebuild your credit immediately after a bankruptcy as it will take time and the consistency of ongoing creditworthiness. This can only be established through multiple actions of repaying bills on time and staying creditworthy.

How Many Years Does It Take For A Person To Rebuild Their Credit After Bankruptcy?

It depends on how hard a person tries to rebuild their credit after a bankruptcy – if a person actively proceeds to rebuild their credit post-bankruptcy then within 12-24 months one should see improvement in their credit profile.

What Are The Best Ways To Get New Credit After Bankruptcy?

The best way to gain new credit after a bankruptcy is to apply for a secured credit card. A secured credit card requires a cash deposit into a savings account to be used as security. Payments will be reported to the credit bureaus and on-time payments will have a positive effect on your credit score. Some credit card companies that offer credit immediately after bankruptcy may charge higher interest rates and steeper late fees. So, you should weigh your options carefully as you begin to restore your credit after bankruptcy. Another way to quickly rebuild your credit following bankruptcy is to become an authorized user to another person's existing credit card.

Does Applying For Credit And Being Denied Further Harm My Credit?

It depends. Generally speaking, being denied for credit after bankruptcy will not further harm your credit so long as it is not excessive. It just means that you have a little more work to do. Remember, after bankruptcy you have been given a fresh start and you must work to rebuild your credit. The only way you can do that is to actually apply for credit. But you want to go about it the smart way. You will need to do some research and get some additional training on how to rebuild your credit. On the web, you will find a wealth of information and numerous websites dedicated to helping people recover from bankruptcy and rebuild their credit. There are articles, seminars, and how-to coaching designed to help you get back on track and build the stellar credit profile you dream of. The first and best resource is your bankruptcy attorney.

At Smith Law Firm, we keep a list of resources that will help you get back on track. Even if you choose not to file bankruptcy right now, we still can offer you some resources that can help you improve your credit now and in the future.

What Is The Difference Between Secured Credit And Unsecured Credit?

There are two types of secured credit. The first is a secured credit card, which is a credit line that is secured by a savings deposit account. This is one of the easiest ways to begin re-establishing credit after a bankruptcy. Ask your bank if they offer a secured card and check online because many of the major credit card companies offer secured credit cards.

Mortgage loans and auto loans are also forms of secured credit. Since you are offering a lien against your real estate or title against your vehicle as collateral to secure the loans, they are considered secured credit.

Unsecured credit means that you do not have to pledge any collateral against a loan, credit card, or line of credit. Examples of unsecured credit include student loans, personal loans, and department store credit cards.

If I Get a Credit Card, Should I Use It Or Keep Balance At Zero?

In order to rebuild your credit and improve you credit score following a bankruptcy, you will need to use your credit cards. Credit scores are determined, in part, by what is referred to as the credit utilization rate. This is the current balance divided by your available credit line. You should try to keep your balances at or below 30% of your credit limit. Studies show that people with the highest credit scores are those who keep their utilization rates anywhere from 1% to 30%. But it is important that you continue to make timely and full payments each month. Be smart with credit card usage. Know what your monthly payment will be and make sure you keep your balance low enough to make sure you can afford to make the full payment. This will go a long way in helping you rebuild the best credit profile you can after bankruptcy.

Why And When Should I Review My Credit Score After A Bankruptcy?

You should take stock of your credit report directly after a bankruptcy so that you can make a practical assessment of what happened to create the situation that you found yourself in and to find lines of alternative credit. You will

need to know who you had credit with before and try to find new companies to provide lines of credit in the future, as they would be more likely to extend new credit than a creditor you previously defaulted on. Your credit report will show the current status on each line of credit. You or anyone viewing your credit report will be able to tell which accounts were discharged in bankruptcy and which ones were successfully repaid by you.

What Are The Best Ways To Use Credit After A Bankruptcy?

Be sure to use credit responsibly and wisely following bankruptcy. Avoid taking out loans on things that you do not need. Also avoid opening lines of credit for discounts and rebates. However, you can benefit from new credit cards, even if they are at a higher rate of interest and secured with a cash deposit. Within the first year after bankruptcy discharge, you should be able to qualify for a car loan. After two years you could qualify for a home mortgage. If you need one or both of those things, after a bankruptcy is a great time to get them since you will have no debt on your record and will therefore be looked upon as creditworthy.

Will Filing Bankruptcy Separately From My Spouse Show Up On His Or Her Credit Report?

Your separate bankruptcy filing will not show up on your spouse's credit report in most cases. If you have any joint accounts with your spouse, you need to decide if you want to have your spouse repay those debts once discharged. If so, discuss with the creditor how they will report that on both of your credit reports. Also, remember that the creditor can still pursue collection activities against your spouse, but not you. Talk to your bankruptcy attorney for advice on how to handle joint credit accounts. Your attorney will advise you if it is best to reaffirm joint credit or include them in your dischargeable debts.

What Are Credit Repair Scams that I Should Avoid?

If you enter into any agreement with a credit repair agency you should carefully review the company and the contract prior to signing or agreeing to anything. Some credit repair agencies charge exorbitant fees when they are not able to do anything to improve your score. Moreover, it is possible for a credit repair agency to make matters worse for the debtor if laws are violated in an attempt to repair one's credit. Keep in mind you must be told that you have a right to dispute any item on your credit rating that adversely affects it which you believe should not be there. Also, a credit repair company is not allowed to charge a fee unless and until work is performed to help repair your credit.

How Can Filing Bankruptcy Actually Help My Credit?

Filing for bankruptcy can definitely be of a benefit to a person's credit since it effectively wipes all debt away and creates a clean slate for a person. The person is then able to build up their credit again where they most likely would not have had that option previously.

What Are Some Other Basic Tips I Can Use That Will Help Me Repair My Credit After A Bankruptcy?

The best tips to remember to rebuild your credit score after a bankruptcy are:

Make consistent and on time payments on any debt that you reaffirm, and also make on-time and full payments on your rent or mortgage and utility bill payments.

Apply for a secured credit card, use it wisely, and make the full monthly payment on time, on a consistent basis. Also, be aware of your utilization rate – keeping your balances below 30% of the available spend amount.

Consider taking out an auto or car loan within a year after bankruptcy. This is the gateway to rebuilding your credit score so that you can qualify for a mortgage loan.

Finally, if your goal is to become a homeowner, apply for a mortgage loan within 12-24 months after bankruptcy discharge.

If you follow this simple formula, you will be on the way to rebuilding great credit to obtain the things you want and need for yourself and family including a home, a car, and education for your children.

Some final thoughts...

The decision to file bankruptcy is often a long and difficult journey filled with emotion, apprehension, and finally relief. No matter how much debt you have, or the reason why it has reached this point, you should feel comfortable with your decision to file bankruptcy. That is why I wrote this book, to help you sort through the issues, the thoughts, the pain associated with financial stress and the weight of debt.

At the Smith Law Firm, our job is to help you and your family with one of the most critical life decisions. Not only are we experienced in bankruptcy law, but we know about life. We know that people's situations change every day, many times by no fault of their own, and they find themselves in need of help. Job loss, major illness, death, and many other situations arise that can lead to a drastic change in your financial situation. That is why we are here, to help you when you and your family need it the most.

If you have been considering filing bankruptcy, or just have questions about your financial situation, managing debt, dealing with creditor harassment, or how to find the credit counseling and education to help you get back on track without filing for bankruptcy give us a call today. We will point you in the right direction and help you get back on track.

Disclaimer

This publication is intended to be informational only. No legal advice is being given, and no attorney-client relationship is intended to be created by reading this material. If you are facing legal issues, whether criminal or civil, seek professional legal counsel to get your questions answered.

The Smith Law Firm, PC

Ames Office
137 Lynn Avenue
Ames, IA 50014
(515) 817-1339
www.shawnsmithlaw.com

Des Moines Office
699 Walnut Street
Suite 400, 4th Floor
Des Moines, Iowa 50309
(855) 451-1260

Made in the USA
Monee, IL
05 November 2026

67386565R00036